ASAP_Kw[illegible]tus

2D Bangz
@soundcloud

HOLT ELEMENTS OF LITERATURE

Sixth Course

ESSENTIALS OF BRITISH AND WORLD LITERATURE

HOLT

ELEMENTS OF LITERATURE®

Sixth Course

ESSENTIALS OF BRITISH AND WORLD LITERATURE

HOLT, RINEHART AND WINSTON

A Harcourt Education Company

Orlando • **Austin** • New York • San Diego • Toronto • London

Cover
Photo Credits: (Inset) *Houses of Parliament from Westminster Bridge,* 1906 by André Derain (1880–1954). Oil on canvas. 73.6 x 92 cm. © The Cleveland Museum of Art, Leonard C. Hanna, Jr. Fund, 1983.67. © 2005 Artists Rights Society (ARS), New York/ADAGP, Paris. (Background) Big Ben. © Jon Bower/Alamy.

Requests for permission to make copies of any part of the work should be mailed to the following address: Permissions Department, Holt, Rinehart and Winston, 10801 N. MoPac Expressway, Building 3, Austin, Texas 78759-5415.

Acknowledgments appear on pages 1485–1487, which are an extension of the copyright page.

Printed in the United States of America

ISBN 0-03-042419-4 2 3 4 5 048 10 09 08 07 06

Program Authors

Dr. Kylene Beers is the senior program author for *Elements of Literature*. A former middle school teacher who is now a senior reading researcher in the School Development program at Yale University, Dr. Beers has turned her commitment to helping struggling readers into the major focus of her research, writing, speaking, and teaching. She is the author of *When Kids Can't Read: What Teachers Can Do* and *Aliteracy: The Glitch in Becoming a Nation of Readers*. From 1999 to 2006, she was the editor of the National Council of Teachers of English (NCTE) literacy journal *Voices from the Middle*. Additionally, Dr. Beers is the co-editor of *Into Focus: Understanding and Creating Middle School Readers*. Having authored chapters in numerous books and articles in *English Journal, Journal of Adolescent and Adult Literacy, School Library Journal, Middle Matters,* and *Voices from the Middle,* she is a recognized authority on struggling readers, who speaks both nationally and internationally. Dr. Beers has served as the chair of the National Adolescent Literacy Coalition (2005–2007) and has served as a member of the review boards for *English Journal, The ALAN Review,* the Special Interest Group on Adolescent Literature of the International Reading Association, and the Assembly on Literature for Adolescents of the NCTE. She is the 2001 recipient of the Richard W. Halle Award given by NCTE for outstanding contributions to middle school literacy.

Dr. Lee Odell helped establish the pedagogical framework for writing, listening, and speaking for *Elements of Literature*. Dr. Odell is Professor of Composition Theory and Research and, since 1996, Director of the Writing Program at Rensselaer Polytechnic Institute. He began his career teaching English in middle and high schools. More recently he has worked with teachers in grades k–12 to establish a program that involves students from all disciplines in writing across the curriculum and for communities outside their classrooms. Dr. Odell's most recent book (with Charles R. Cooper) is *Evaluating Writing: The Role of Teacher's Knowledge About Text, Learning, and Culture*. He is past chair of the Conference on College Composition and Communication and of NCTE's Assembly for Research.

Writers

John Malcolm Brinnin, author of six volumes of poetry that have received many prizes and awards, was a member of the American Academy and Institute of Arts and Letters. He was a critic of poetry, a biographer of poets, and for a number of years, director of New York's famous Poetry Center. His teaching career included terms at Vassar College, the University of Connecticut, and Boston University, where he succeeded Robert Lowell as Professor of Creative Writing and Contemporary Letters. In addition to other works, Mr. Brinnin wrote *Dylan Thomas in America: An Intimate Journal* and *Sextet: T. S. Eliot & Truman Capote & Others*.

Claire Miller Colombo received a doctorate in English from the University of Texas at Austin and has taught English at both college and secondary levels. She has been a freelance writer of educational materials since 1990.

Robert DeMaria, Jr., is the Henry Noble MacCracken Professor of English Literature at Vassar College, where he has taught since receiving his doctorate from Rutgers University in 1975. He is an expert on eighteenth-century British literature and has edited the college text *British Literature 1640–1789: An Anthology* (Second Edition, 2001). He has also written three books about Samuel Johnson. Most recently Dr. DeMaria has edited an edition of *Gulliver's Travels*.

Donald Gray is Professor Emeritus of English at Indiana University, Bloomington. Dr. Gray has written essays on Victorian poetry and culture and has served as editor of *College English*.

Harley Henry was Professor of English at Macalester College in St. Paul, Minnesota. He has also been a senior Fulbright lecturer in Zimbabwe and a Redfield Visiting Professor at the University of Chicago. In addition to the Romantic period, his teaching specialties include the literature of Zimbabwe, William Faulkner, American fiction from 1945 to 1960, and fiction about baseball.

Rose Sallberg Kam holds a master's in English from California State University, Sacramento, and a master's in biblical studies from the Graduate Theological Union, Berkeley. She taught secondary English for seventeen years, has been a freelance writer of educational materials for nineteen years, and is the author of *Their Stories, Our Stories: Women of the Bible*.

David Adams Leeming was for many years a Professor of English and Comparative Literature at the University of Connecticut. He is the author of several books on mythology, including *Mythology: The Voyage of the Hero; The World of Myth;* and *Encyclopedia of Creation Myths*. For several years, Dr. Leeming taught English at Robert College in Istanbul, Turkey. He also served as secretary and assistant to the writer James Baldwin in New York and Istanbul. He has published the biographies *James Baldwin* and *Amazing Grace: A Life of Beauford Delaney*.

John Leggett is a novelist, biographer, and former teacher. He went to the Writers' Workshop at the University of Iowa in the spring of 1969. In 1970, he assumed temporary charge of the program, and for the next seventeen years he was its director. Mr. Leggett's novels include *Wilder Stone, The Gloucester Branch, Who Took the Gold Away?, Gulliver House*, and *Making Believe*. He is also the author of the highly acclaimed biography *Ross and Tom: Two American Tragedies* and of a biography of William Saroyan, *A Daring Young Man*. Mr. Leggett lives in Napa Valley, California.

C. F. Main was for many years Professor of English at Rutgers University in New Brunswick, New Jersey. He was the editor of *Poems: Wadsworth Handbook and Anthology* and wrote reviews and articles on sixteenth-, seventeenth-, and eighteenth-century literature.

Fannie Safier, a former teacher, has written and edited language arts materials for over thirty-five years.

Mairead Stack has a master's degree in English from New York University. A former teacher, she has edited and written educational materials for literature and language arts for more than twenty years.

Senior Program Consultant

Carol Jago teaches English at Santa Monica High School, in Santa Monica, and directs the California Reading and Literature Project at UCLA. Her classroom experience began with middle school and has included journalism, remedial reading and writing, and honors and advanced placement. She has written a weekly education column for the *Los Angeles Times* and edits the quarterly journal of the California Association of Teachers of English, *California English*. She is the author of several books, including a series on contemporary writers in the classroom: *Alice Walker in the Classroom*, *Nikki Giovanni in the Classroom*, and *Sandra Cisneros in the Classroom*. She is also the author of *With Rigor for All: Teaching the Classics to Contemporary Students; Beyond Standards: Excellence in the High School English Classroom; Cohesive Writing: Why Concept Is Not Enough; Classics in the Classroom: Designing Accessible Literature Lessons;* and *Papers, Papers, Papers: An English Teacher's Survival Guide.*

ADVISORS

Cynthia A. Arceneaux
Administrative Coordinator
Office of Deputy Superintendent, Instructional Services
Los Angeles Unified School District
Los Angeles, California

Dr. Julie M.T. Chan
Director of Literacy Instruction
Newport-Mesa Unified School District
Costa Mesa, California

Al Desmarais
English Department Chair and Curriculum Specialist in Language Arts
El Toro High School
Saddleback Valley Unified School District
Lake Forest, California

José M. Ibarra-Tiznado
ELL Program Coordinator
Bassett Unified School District
La Puente, California

Dr. Ronald Klemp
Instructor
California State University, Northridge
Northridge, California

Fern M. Sheldon
K–12 Curriculum and Instruction Specialist
Rowland Unified School District
Rowland Heights, California

Jim Shields
Instructor
El Toro High School
Saddleback Valley Unified School District
Lake Forest, California

CRITICAL REVIEWERS

Elmire C. Budak
Lynwood High School
Lynwood, California

Paulette Dewey
Toledo Early College High School
University of Toledo—Scott Park Campus
Toledo, Ohio

Matthew Falk
John A. Rowland High School
Rowland Unified School District
Rowland Heights, California

Terry Filippo
Pendleton High School / Clemson University
Pendleton, South Carolina

R. E. Fisher
Westlake High School
Atlanta, Georgia

Robert V. Gardner
Chaparral High School
Temecula, California

Janice Gauthier
Everett High School
Everett, Massachusetts

Sandra Gilligan
Passaic High School
Passaic, New Jersey

Victor Jaccarino
Herricks High School
New Hyde Park, New York

Diane M. Jackson
Washington Preparatory High School
Los Angeles, California

Barbara Kimbrough
Kane Area High School
Kane, Pennsylvania

Dr. Louisa Kramer-Vida
Oyster Bay-East Norwich SD
Oyster Bay, New York

Martin P. Mushik
Covina High School
Covina, California

Brenda Scheidler
Evansville-Vanderburgh School Corp.
Evansville, Indiana

Mary Ellen Snodgrass
Hickory High School
Hickory, North Carolina

Elaine Sorrell
Marina High School
Huntington Beach, California

David Trimble
Norwin High School
N. Huntingdon, Pennsylvania

Donna Walthour
Greensburg Salem High School
Greensburg, Pennsylvania

John R. Williamson
Highlands High School
Fort Thomas, Kentucky

FIELD-TEST PARTICIPANTS

Barbara A. Briggs
Barberton High School
Barberton, Ohio

Annette Dade
West Orange High School
West Orange, New Jersey

Robert V. Gardner
Chaparral High School
Temecula, California

Bobbye Sykes-Perkins
Luther Burbank High School
Sacramento, California

John R. Williamson
Highlands High School
Fort Thomas, Kentucky

CONTENTS IN BRIEF

COLLECTION 1

The Anglo-Saxons: 449–1066 1

Connecting to World Literature Epics: Stories on a Grand Scale ... 54

Reflecting on the Literary Period The Anglo-Saxons 83

Writing Workshop Writing a Descriptive Essay 96

COLLECTION 2

The Middle Ages: 1066–1485 111

Connecting to World Literature The Frame Story: A Tale Linking Tales 191

Reflecting on the Literary Period The Middle Ages 225

Writing Workshop Reporting Literary Research 240

COLLECTION 3

The Renaissance: 1485–1660 269

Comparing Points of View Education and Equality 358

Connecting to World Literature Worlds of Wisdom: Wisdom Literature 382

Reflecting on the Literary Period The Renaissance 529

Writing Workshop Analyzing Literature 542

COLLECTION 4

The Restoration and the Eighteenth Century: 1660–1800 559

Connecting to World Literature The Sting of Satire 614

Comparing Points of View Women's Rights 634

Reflecting on the Literary Period The Restoration and the Eighteenth Century 651

Writing Workshop Writing a Literary Essay 684

COLLECTION 5

The Romantic Period: 1798–1832 701

Connecting to World Literature Tanka and Haiku 749

Connecting to World Literature The Golden Age of Chinese Poetry 811

Reflecting on the Literary Period The Romantic Period 839
Writing Workshop Writing a Reflective Essay 856

COLLECTION 6
The Victorian Period: 1832–1901 873
Connecting to World Literature The Rise of Realism 946
Reflecting on the Literary Period The Victorian Period 983
Writing Workshop Comparing and Contrasting Literature 1002

COLLECTION 7
The Modern World: 1900 to the Present 1017
A WORLD AT WAR 1037
Comparing Points of View The Holocaust 1050
Mini-Workshop Writing a Persuasive Essay 1101

CLASHES OF CULTURE 1103
Comparing Points of View Colonialism 1114
Mini-Workshop Analyzing Nonfiction 1159

DISCOVERIES AND TRANSFORMATIONS 1161
Mini-Workshop Writing a Short Story 1249

OURSELVES AMONG OTHERS 1251
Comparing Points of View Human Rights 1306
Reflecting on the Literary Period The Modern World 1329
Media Workshop Analyzing and Using Media 1344

RESOURCE CENTER
Reading Matters 1363
The World of Work 1377
Writer's Handbook 1383
Test Smarts 1395
Handbook of Literary and Historical Terms 1411
Language Handbook 1435
Glossary 1473
Spanish Glossary 1479

Maps
The British Isles A54
Map of the World A56

COLLECTION 1

The Anglo-Saxons 449–1066

SONGS OF ANCIENT HEROES

TIME LINE 2

POLITICAL AND SOCIAL MILESTONES 4

INTRODUCTION TO THE LITERARY PERIOD
David Adams Leeming — **The Anglo-Saxons: 449–1066** 6

Beowulf *(Introduction)* 18
Anonymous — *from* **Beowulf** *translated by* Burton Raffel .... EPIC 20
The Monster Grendel 21
The Arrival of the Hero 24
Unferth's Challenge 26
The Battle with Grendel 31
The Monster's Mother 36
John Gardner — *from* **Grendel** / CONNECTION .... NOVEL 39
Howard G. Chua-Eoan — **Life in 999: A Grim Struggle** / CONNECTION .... MAGAZINE ARTICLE 40

Anonymous — *from* **Beowulf** *translated by* Seamus Heaney .... EPIC
The Final Battle 43
Ellen Ashdown — **The Fury of the Northmen** / CONNECTION .... ARTICLE 49

Connecting to World Literature
Epics: Stories on a Grand Scale *by* David Adams Leeming ... 54
Anonymous (MESOPOTAMIA) — *from* **Gilgamesh: A Verse Narrative** *retold by* Herbert Mason .... EPIC 57
Homer (GREECE) — *the* **Iliad,** *from* **Book 22: The Death of Hector** *translated by* Robert Fagles .... EPIC 66
C. W. Ceram — **Trojan Gold** *from* **Gods, Graves, and Scholars** / CONNECTION ...... HISTORY 77

Reflecting on the Literary Period
The Anglo-Saxons: 449–1066 83

Bede — *from* **A History of the English Church and People** *translated by* Leo Sherley-Price .... HISTORY 84

Anonymous — **The Seafarer** *translated by* Burton Raffel .... POEM 87

Anonymous — **The Wife's Lament** *translated by* Richard Hamer .... POEM 92

READ ON *For Independent Reading* 95

WRITING WORKSHOP *Writing a Descriptive Essay* 96

PREPARING FOR STANDARDIZED TESTS Collection Skills Review

COMPARING LITERATURE

Anonymous — *from* **The Wanderer** *translated by* Burton Raffel .... POEM 104

Alfred, Lord Tennyson — **Break, Break, Break** .... POEM 106

VOCABULARY SKILLS 108

WRITING SKILLS 109

COLLECTION 2

The Middle Ages 1066–1485

THE TALES THEY TOLD

TIME LINE 112

POLITICAL AND SOCIAL MILESTONES 114

INTRODUCTION TO THE LITERARY PERIOD

David Adams Leeming — **The Middle Ages: 1066–1485** 116

Anonymous — **Lord Randall** .... BALLAD 130

Anonymous — **Get Up and Bar the Door** .... BALLAD 132

The Canterbury Tales: Snapshot of an Age *(Introduction)* 137

Geoffrey Chaucer — *from* **The Canterbury Tales** *translated by* Nevill Coghill .... NARRATIVE POEM

The Prologue 140

from **The Pardoner's Tale** 167

from **The Wife of Bath's Tale** 177

Connecting to World Literature

The Frame Story: A Tale Linking Tales *by* David Adams Leeming 191

Panchatantra (INDIA) — **Right-Mind and Wrong-Mind** *translated by* Arthur William Ryder .... FABLE 194

The Thousand and One Nights (ARABIA) — *from* **The Third Voyage of Sindbad the Sailor** *translated by* N. J. Dawood .... STORY 201

Giovanni Boccaccio (ITALY) — **Federigo's Falcon** *from the* **Decameron** *translated by* Mark Musa *and* Peter Bondanella .... STORY 208

Sir Thomas Malory — *from* **The Day of Destiny** *from* **Le Morte d'Arthur** *retold by* Keith Baines .... ROMANCE NARRATIVE 215

Reflecting on the Literary Period

The Middle Ages: 1066–1485 225

Anonymous — **Edward, Edward** .... BALLAD 226

Anonymous — *from* **Sir Gawain and the Green Knight** *translated by* John Gardner .... ROMANCE NARRATIVE 229

READ ON *For Independent Reading* 239

WRITING WORKSHOP *Reporting Literary Research* 240

LISTENING AND SPEAKING WORKSHOP *Presenting Literary Research* 260

PREPARING FOR STANDARDIZED TESTS Collection Skills Review

COMPARING LITERATURE

Anonymous **The Twa Corbies** .... BALLAD 262

Alexander Pushkin **Raven doth to raven fly** *translated by* Walter Arndt .... POEM 263

VOCABULARY SKILLS 266

WRITING SKILLS 267

COLLECTION 3

The Renaissance 1485–1660

A FLOURISH OF GENIUS

TIME LINE ... 270

POLITICAL AND SOCIAL MILESTONES ... 272

INTRODUCTION TO THE LITERARY PERIOD

C. F. Main — **The Renaissance: 1485–1660** ... 274

Christopher Marlowe — **The Passionate Shepherd to His Love** ... POEM 293

Sir Walter Raleigh — **The Nymph's Reply to the Shepherd** ... POEM 297

Robert Herrick — **To the Virgins, to Make Much of Time** ... POEM 299

Andrew Marvell — **To His Coy Mistress** ... POEM 303

Joseph Papp *and* Elizabeth Kirkland — **Give Us This Day Our Daily Bread** / CONNECTION ... HISTORY 305

Shakespeare's Sonnets: The Mysteries of Love *(Introduction)* ... 311

Francesco Petrarch — **Sonnet 42** *translated by* Joseph Auslander ... SONNET 312

William Shakespeare — **Sonnet 18** ... SONNET 313

Sonnet 29 ... SONNET 314

Sonnet 30 ... SONNET 316

Sonnet 71 ... SONNET 317

Sonnet 73 ... SONNET 318

Sonnet 116 ... SONNET 319

Sonnet 130 ... SONNET 320

Louise Labé — **Sonnet 23** *translated by* Willis Barnstone ... SONNET 321

William Shakespeare — **Blow, Blow, Thou Winter Wind** ... SONG 322

Fear No More the Heat o' the Sun ... SONG 324

Full Fathom Five ... SONG 326

FAMOUS SHAKESPEAREAN SPEECHES

To be, or not to be *from* **Hamlet** ... SOLILOQUY 328

Tomorrow, and tomorrow, and tomorrow *from* **The Tragedy of Macbeth** ... SOLILOQUY 331

Saint Crispin's Day Speech *from* **Henry V** ... SPEECH 332

Our revels now are ended *from* **The Tempest** ... SPEECH 334

Author	Title	Genre	Page
John Donne	**Song**	POEM	337
	A Valediction: Forbidding Mourning	POEM	340
	Meditation 17	MEDITATION	343
	Death be not proud	SONNET	348
Margaret Edson	*from* **W;t** / CONNECTION	DRAMA	350
Ben Jonson	**On My First Son**	POEM	354
	Song: To Celia	POEM	356
	Comparing Points of View Education and Equality		358
	Main Reading		
Francis Bacon	**Of Studies**	ESSAY	360
	Axioms *from the* **Essays** *by* Francis Bacon / PRIMARY SOURCE	AXIOMS	363
	Connected Readings		
	PUBLIC DOCUMENT		
Queen Elizabeth I	**Tilbury Speech**	SPEECH	366
	PUBLIC DOCUMENT		
Margaret Cavendish, duchess of Newcastle	*from* **Female Orations**	DEBATE	368
	The King James Bible (1611): A Masterpiece by a Committee *(Introduction)*		372
	Psalms: Worship Through Poetry *(Introduction)*		373
King James Bible	**Psalm 23**	PSALM	374
	Psalm 137	PSALM	376
	The Parable of the Prodigal Son	PARABLE	378

Connecting to World Literature

Worlds of Wisdom: Wisdom Literature 382

Koran ARABIA — **Night** *translated by* N. J. Dawood .... SACRED TEXT 385

Bhagavad-Gita INDIA — *from* **Philosophy and Spiritual Discipline** *translated by* Barbara Stoler Miller .... SACRED TEXT 387

Buddhist Traditional JAPAN — **Zen Parables** *compiled by* Paul Reps .... PARABLES 389

Confucius CHINA — *from* **The Analects of Confucius** *translated and annotated by* Arthur Waley .... MAXIMS 391

Lao Tzu CHINA — *from the* **Tao Te Ching** *translated by* Stephen Mitchell .... SACRED TEXT 392

Tao Traditional CHINA — **Taoist Anecdotes** *translated and edited by* Moss Roberts .... ANECDOTES 393

Saadi PERSIA — **Sayings of Saadi** *translated by* Idries Shah .... AXIOMS 394

African Traditional AFRICA — **African Proverbs** *compiled by* Charlotte *and* Wolf Leslau .... PROVERBS 395

Paradise Lost: Milton's Epic *(Introduction)* 399

John Milton — **The Fall of Satan** *from* **Paradise Lost** .... EPIC 401

When I consider how my light is spent .... SONNET 415

John Bunyan — *from* **The Pilgrim's Progress** .... ALLEGORY 419

RENAISSANCE DRAMA

	The Renaissance Theater *(Introduction)*	426
	***The Tragedy of Macbeth:* The Sources of the Play**	435
William Shakespeare	**The Tragedy of Macbeth** ... TRAGEDY	438
	Act I	440
	Act II	457
Thomas De Quincey	*from* **On the Knocking at the Gate in *Macbeth*** / CONNECTION ... ESSAY	468
William Shakespeare	**Act III**	472
	Act IV	490
	Act V	508
Richard Armour	**Macbeth and the Witches** / CONNECTION ... PARODY	524

Reflecting on the Literary Period

	The Renaissance: 1485–1660	529
Sir Thomas Wyatt	**Whoso List to Hunt** ... SONNET	530
Edmund Spenser	*from* **Amoretti**	
	Sonnet 30 ... SONNET	532
	Sonnet 75 ... SONNET	534
Sir John Suckling	**Why So Pale and Wan, Fond Lover?** ... POEM	535
Richard Lovelace	**To Lucasta, on Going to the Wars** ... POEM	537
	To Althea, from Prison ... POEM	538

	READ ON *For Independent Reading*	541
	WRITING WORKSHOP *Analyzing Literature*	542
	LISTENING AND SPEAKING WORKSHOP *Reciting Literature*	550
	PREPARING FOR STANDARDIZED TESTS Collection Skills Review	
	COMPARING LITERATURE	
Pierre de Ronsard	**When You Are Old** *translated by* Humbert Wolfe ... POEM	552
William Butler Yeats	**When You Are Old** ... POEM	553
	VOCABULARY SKILLS	556
	WRITING SKILLS	557

COLLECTION 4

The Restoration and the Eighteenth Century 1660–1800

THE BEST OF ALL POSSIBLE WORLDS

TIME LINE 560

POLITICAL AND SOCIAL MILESTONES 562

INTRODUCTION TO THE LITERARY PERIOD

C. F. Main — **The Restoration and the Eighteenth Century: 1660–1800** .. 564

Jonathan Swift — **A Modest Proposal** .... ESSAY 580

T. Coraghessan Boyle — **Top of the Food Chain** / CONNECTION .... SHORT STORY 590

Alexander Pope — **Heroic Couplets** .... COUPLETS 598

from **An Essay on Man** .... PHILOSOPHICAL POEM 601

from **The Rape of the Lock** .... MOCK EPIC 603

Connecting to World Literature

The Sting of Satire *by* Robert DeMaria, Jr. 614

Voltaire (FRANCE) — *from* **Candide** *translated by* Richard Aldington .... NOVEL 618

Miguel de Cervantes (SPAIN) — *from* **Don Quixote** *translated by* Samuel Putnam .... NOVEL 626

Comparing Points of View Women's Rights 634

Main Reading

PUBLIC DOCUMENT

Mary Wollstonecraft — *from* **A Vindication of the Rights of Woman** .... PLATFORM 637

Connected Readings

Mary, Lady Chudleigh — **To the Ladies** .... POEM 646

Daniel Defoe — *from* **The Education of Women** .... ESSAY 647

Reflecting on the Literary Period

The Restoration and the Eighteenth Century: 1660–1800 651

Jonathan Swift — *from* **Gulliver's Travels** .... NOVEL 652
from **Part 1: A Voyage to Lilliput** 653
from **Part 2: A Voyage to Brobdingnag** 660

Daniel Defoe — *from* **A Journal of the Plague Year** .... NOVEL 663

Samuel Johnson — *from* **A Dictionary of the English Language** .... DEFINITIONS 667

James Boswell — *from* **The Life of Samuel Johnson** .... BIOGRAPHY 670

Thomas Gray — **Elegy Written in a Country Churchyard** .... ELEGY 676

READ ON *For Independent Reading* 683

WRITING WORKSHOP *Writing a Literary Essay* 684

LISTENING AND SPEAKING WORKSHOP
Presenting a Literary Response 692

PREPARING FOR STANDARDIZED TESTS Collection Skills Review

COMPARING LITERATURE

Tacitus — *from* **The Burning of Rome** *from* **The Annals**
translated by George Gilbert Ramsay .... ANNAL 694

Samuel Pepys — *from* **The Diary of Samuel Pepys** .... DIARY 695

VOCABULARY SKILLS 698

WRITING SKILLS 699

COLLECTION 5

The Romantic Period 1798–1832

THE QUEST FOR TRUTH AND BEAUTY

TIME LINE 702

POLITICAL AND SOCIAL MILESTONES 704

INTRODUCTION TO THE LITERARY PERIOD

Harley Henry — **The Romantic Period: 1798–1832** 706

Blake's Poems: Innocence to Experience *(Introduction)* 719

William Blake — **The Tyger** .... POEM 720

Charles Lamb — **"Blake Is a Real Name . . ."** / PRIMARY SOURCE .... LETTER 722

William Blake — **The Lamb** .... POEM 723

The Chimney Sweeper *from* **Songs of Innocence** .... POEM 725

The Chimney Sweeper *from* **Songs of Experience** .... POEM 727

PUBLIC DOCUMENT

Peter Smart — *from* **Evidence Given Before the Sadler Committee** / PRIMARY SOURCE .... TESTIMONY 728

William Blake — **A Poison Tree** .... POEM 731

William Wordsworth — **Lines Composed a Few Miles Above Tintern Abbey** .... POEM 735

Composed upon Westminster Bridge .... SONNET 743

The World Is Too Much with Us .... SONNET 745

Connecting to World Literature

Tanka and Haiku 749

Tanka Poets, JAPAN — **Tanka** *translated by* Geoffrey Bownas *and* Anthony Thwaite .... TANKA 751

Haiku Poets, JAPAN — **Haiku** *translated by* Harold G. Henderson, Peter Beilenson, *and* Harry Behn .... HAIKU 755

Samuel Taylor Coleridge	**Kubla Khan**	POEM	758
	The Rime of the Ancient Mariner	NARRATIVE POEM	762
	Coleridge Describes His Addiction *by* Samuel Taylor Coleridge / PRIMARY SOURCE	LETTER	787
Bruce Chatwin	*from* **In Patagonia** / CONNECTION	TRAVEL BOOK	788
George Gordon, Lord Byron	**She Walks in Beauty**	POEM	794
	from **Childe Harold's Pilgrimage, Canto IV**	NARRATIVE POEM	796
Percy Bysshe Shelley	**Ozymandias**	SONNET	802
	Ode to the West Wind	ODE	805

Connecting to World Literature
The Golden Age of Chinese Poetry 811

Tu Fu CHINA
Jade Flower Palace *translated by* Kenneth Rexroth .... POEM 815
Night Thoughts Afloat *translated by* Arthur Cooper ..... POEM 817

Li Po CHINA
Quiet Night Thoughts *translated by* Arthur Cooper ...... POEM 820
Question and Answer Among the Mountains *translated by* Robert Kotewall *and* Norman L. Smith .... POEM 821
Letter to His Two Small Children *translated by* Arthur Cooper .... POEM 822

John Keats
On First Looking into Chapman's Homer .... SONNET 825
When I Have Fears .... SONNET 827
Keats's Last Letter *by* John Keats / PRIMARY SOURCE ..... LETTER 829
Ode to a Nightingale .... ODE 830
Ode on a Grecian Urn .... ODE 835

Reflecting on the Literary Period
The Romantic Period: 1798–1832 839

Robert Burns
To a Mouse .... POEM 840
To a Louse .... POEM 843

William Wordsworth
from **Ode: Intimations of Immortality** .... ODE 846

Percy Bysshe Shelley
To a Skylark .... POEM 849

READ ON *For Independent Reading* 855

WRITING WORKSHOP *Writing a Reflective Essay* 856

LISTENING AND SPEAKING WORKSHOP
Presenting a Reflection 864

PREPARING FOR STANDARDIZED TESTS Collection Skills Review
COMPARING LITERATURE
William Blake **London** .... POEM 866
Derek Walcott **The Virgins** .... POEM 867
VOCABULARY SKILLS 870
WRITING SKILLS 871

COLLECTION 6

The Victorian Period 1832–1901

PARADOX AND PROGRESS

TIME LINE 874

POLITICAL AND SOCIAL MILESTONES 876

INTRODUCTION TO THE LITERARY PERIOD

Donald Gray — The Victorian Period: 1832–1901 878

Alfred, Lord Tennyson — The Lady of Shalott .... NARRATIVE POEM 895

Ulysses .... POEM 903

Robert Browning — My Last Duchess .... DRAMATIC MONOLOGUE 908

Julia Markus — Scenes from a Modern Marriage / CONNECTION .... NEWS FEATURE 911

Elizabeth Barrett Browning — **Sonnet 43** .... SONNET 914

Gerard Manley Hopkins — **Pied Beauty** .... POEM 917

Matthew Arnold — **Dover Beach** .... POEM 921

A. E. Housman — **To an Athlete Dying Young** .... POEM 926

Daniel Pool — **Death and Other Grave Matters** / CONNECTION .... HISTORY 928

Rudyard Kipling — **The Mark of the Beast** .... SHORT STORY 931

Connecting to World Literature

The Rise of Realism 946

Leo Tolstoy (RUSSIA) — **How Much Land Does a Man Need?** *translated by* Louise *and* Aylmer Maude .... SHORT STORY 950

Anton Chekhov (RUSSIA) — **The Bet** *translated by* Constance Garnett .... SHORT STORY 966

Guy de Maupassant (FRANCE) — **The Jewels** *translated by* Roger Colet .... SHORT STORY 975

Reflecting on the Literary Period

The Victorian Period: 1832–1901 983

Alfred, Lord Tennyson — *from* **In Memoriam A.H.H.** .... ELEGY 984

Crossing the Bar .... POEM 989

Robert Browning — **Porphyria's Lover** .... DRAMATIC MONOLOGUE 990

Thomas Hardy — **The Darkling Thrush** .... POEM 993

Ah, Are You Digging on My Grave? .... POEM 996

A. E. Housman — **When I Was One-and-Twenty** .... POEM 998

READ ON *For Independent Reading* 1001

WRITING WORKSHOP *Comparing and Contrasting Literature* 1002

PREPARING FOR STANDARDIZED TESTS Collection Skills Review

COMPARING LITERATURE

Thomas Hardy — **Drummer Hodge** .... POEM 1010

Arthur Rimbaud — **The Sleeper of the Valley** *translated by* Ludwig Lewisohn .... POEM 1011

VOCABULARY SKILLS 1014

WRITING SKILLS 1015

COLLECTION 7

The Modern World 1900 to the Present

A REMARKABLE DIVERSITY

TIME LINE 1018

POLITICAL AND SOCIAL MILESTONES 1020

INTRODUCTION TO THE LITERARY PERIOD

John Leggett *and* **David Adams Leeming** — **The Modern World: 1900 to the Present** 1022

A WORLD AT WAR

Wilfred Owen ENGLAND — **Dulce et Decorum Est** .... POEM 1039

Siegfried Sassoon ENGLAND — **The Rear-Guard** / CONNECTION .... POEM 1041

T. S. Eliot AMERICA / ENGLAND — **The Hollow Men** .... POEM 1044

Comparing Points of View The Holocaust 1050

Main Reading

Primo Levi ITALY — **On the Bottom** *from* **Survival in Auschwitz** *translated by* Stuart Woolf .... MEMOIR 1052

Connected Readings

Marguerite Duras FRANCE — *from* **The War** *translated by* Barbara Bray .... MEMOIR 1058

Elie Wiesel ROMANIA — **Never Shall I Forget** .... POEM 1062

The United States Holocaust Memorial Museum — **Kristallnacht** / CONNECTION .... WEB PAGE 1064

PUBLIC DOCUMENT

Winston Churchill ENGLAND — **Blood, Sweat, and Tears** .... SPEECH 1067

Yasunari Kawabata JAPAN — **The Silver Fifty-Sen Pieces** *translated by* Lane Dunlop *and* J. Martin Holman ... SHORT STORY 1072

Graham Greene ENGLAND — **The Destructors** .... SHORT STORY 1080

Ben Okri NIGERIA — **In the Shadow of War** .... SHORT STORY 1093

Wisława Szymborska POLAND — **The End and the Beginning** *translated by* Stanislaw Baranczak *and* Clare Cavanagh / CONNECTION .... POEM 1098

Mini-Workshop Writing a Persuasive Essay 1101

Magritte

CLASHES OF CULTURE

Virginia Woolf ENGLAND — **Shakespeare's Sister** *from* **A Room of One's Own** ..... ESSAY 1105

Comparing Points of View Colonialism 1114

Main Readings

George Orwell ENGLAND — **Shooting an Elephant** ..... ESSAY 1116

Doris Lessing ZIMBABWE — **No Witchcraft for Sale** ..... SHORT STORY 1126

Connected Readings

PUBLIC DOCUMENT

Joseph Chamberlain ENGLAND — **"I Believe in a British Empire"** ..... SPEECH 1134

PUBLIC DOCUMENT

Jawaharlal Nehru INDIA — **"The Noble Mansion of Free India"** ..... SPEECH 1137

Nadine Gordimer SOUTH AFRICA — **Once upon a Time** ..... SHORT STORY 1141

Chinua Achebe NIGERIA — **Marriage Is a Private Affair** ..... SHORT STORY 1148

Wole Soyinka NIGERIA — **Telephone Conversation** ..... POEM 1156

Mini-Workshop Analyzing Nonfiction 1159

DISCOVERIES AND TRANSFORMATIONS

William Butler Yeats IRELAND — **The Second Coming** ..... POEM 1163

The Lake Isle of Innisfree ..... POEM 1166

The Wild Swans at Coole ..... POEM 1169

Rainer Maria Rilke CZECHOSLOVAKIA / AUSTRIA — **The Swan** *translated by* Robert Bly / CONNECTION ..... POEM 1171

James Joyce IRELAND — **Araby** ..... SHORT STORY 1174

D. H. Lawrence ENGLAND — **The Rocking-Horse Winner** ..... SHORT STORY 1186

D. H. Lawrence on Money *by* D. H. Lawrence / PRIMARY SOURCE ..... LETTER 1198

Anna Akhmatova RUSSIA

Lot's Wife *translated by* Richard Wilbur .... POEM 1201

All the unburied ones *translated by* Judith Hemschemeyer .... POEM 1203

I am not one of those who left the land *translated by* Stanley Kunitz .... POEM 1203

Elizabeth Bowen IRELAND

The Demon Lover .... SHORT STORY 1206

Julio Cortázar ARGENTINA

Axolotl *translated by* Paul Blackburn .... SHORT STORY 1217

Jorge Luis Borges ARGENTINA

The Book of Sand *translated by* Andrew Hurley .... SHORT STORY 1225

V. S. Naipaul TRINIDAD

B. Wordsworth .... SHORT STORY 1233

Naguib Mahfouz EGYPT

Half a Day *translated by* Denys Johnson-Davies .... SHORT STORY 1241

Seamus Heaney IRELAND

Digging .... POEM 1246

Mini-Workshop Writing a Short Story 1249

OURSELVES AMONG OTHERS

Katherine Mansfield NEW ZEALAND

The Doll's House .... SHORT STORY 1253

W. H. Auden ENGLAND / AMERICA

Musée des Beaux Arts .... POEM 1264

Gabriela Mistral CHILE

Fear *translated by* Doris Dana .... POEM 1267

Dylan Thomas WALES

Fern Hill .... POEM 1271

Do Not Go Gentle into That Good Night .... POEM 1274

Pablo Neruda CHILE

Sonnet 79 *translated by* Stephen Tapscott .... SONNET 1278

Soneto 79 .... SONETO 1278

R. K. Narayan INDIA

Like the Sun .... SHORT STORY 1282

Anita Desai INDIA

Games at Twilight .... SHORT STORY 1289

Penelope Lively ENGLAND

Next Term, We'll Mash You .... SHORT STORY 1299

Comparing Points of View Human Rights 1306

Main Reading

Ha Jin
CHINA
Saboteur .... SHORT STORY 1308

Connected Readings

United Nations Commission on Human Rights
PUBLIC DOCUMENT
from the **Universal Declaration of Human Rights** .... POLITICAL STATEMENT 1318

Desmond Tutu
SOUTH AFRICA
PUBLIC DOCUMENT
from **The Question of South Africa** .... SPEECH 1320

Aung San Suu Kyi
MYANMAR
PUBLIC DOCUMENT
from **Towards a True Refuge** .... SPEECH 1324

Reflecting on the Literary Period
The Modern World: 1900 to the Present 1329

Rupert Brooke — **The Soldier** .... SONNET 1330

William Butler Yeats — **Sailing to Byzantium** .... POEM 1332

Ted Hughes — **The Horses** .... POEM 1334

Stevie Smith — **Not Waving but Drowning** .... POEM 1337

Harold Pinter — **That's All** .... DRAMA 1339

READ ON *For Independent Reading* 1343

MEDIA WORKSHOP *Analyzing and Using Media* 1344

LISTENING AND SPEAKING WORKSHOP
Presenting and Analyzing Speeches 1352

PREPARING FOR STANDARDIZED TESTS Collection Skills Review

COMPARING LITERATURE

Heinrich Heine — **The Lorelei**
translated by Louis Untermeyer .... POEM 1356

Margaret Atwood — **Siren Song** .... POEM 1357

VOCABULARY SKILLS 1360

WRITING SKILLS 1361

Resource Center

Reading Matters *by* Kylene Beers 1363
When the Text Is Tough 1363
Improving Your Comprehension 1364
Improving Your Reading Rate 1373
Vocabulary Development 1375

The World of Work 1377
Reading 1377
Informative Documents 1377
    Consumer Documents 1377
    Workplace Documents 1378
Persuasive Documents 1379
    Critiquing Persuasive Documents 1379
Writing 1380
Job Applications and Résumés 1380
Workplace Documents 1381
Word-Processing Features 1381
    Integrating Databases, Graphics, and Spreadsheets 1381
    Résumé Format 1381

Writer's Handbook 1383
The Writing Process 1383
Paragraphs 1385
The Writer's Language 1389
Designing Your Writing 1391

Test Smarts *by* Flo Ota De Lange *and* Sheri Henderson 1395
Strategies for Taking Multiple-Choice Tests 1395
Strategies for Taking Writing Tests 1404

Handbook of Literary and Historical Terms 1411

Language Handbook 1435
The Parts of Speech 1436
Agreement 1437
Using Verbs 1439
Using Pronouns 1441
Using Modifiers 1443
Phrases 1444

Clauses 1446
Sentence Structure 1447
Sentence Style 1450
Sentence Combining 1453
Capitalization 1454
Punctuation 1457, 1460
Spelling 1465
Glossary of Usage 1467

Glossary 1473

Spanish Glossary 1479

Acknowledgments 1485

Picture Credits 1488

Index of Skills 1491
Literary Skills 1491
Vocabulary Skills 1493
Reading Skills 1494
Writing Skills 1495
Language (Grammar, Usage, and Mechanics) Skills 1500
Listening and Speaking Skills 1501
Independent Reading 1503

Index of Art 1504

Index of Authors and Titles 1510

SELECTIONS BY ALTERNATIVE THEMES

Selections are listed here in alternative theme groupings.

APPEARANCE VERSUS REALITY

Our revels now are ended
from **The Tempest**
William Shakespeare ... 334

from **Don Quixote**
Miguel de Cervantes ... 626

She Walks in Beauty
George Gordon, Lord Byron ... 794

Ozymandias
Percy Bysshe Shelley ... 802

To a Louse
Robert Burns ... 843

The Lady of Shalott
Alfred, Lord Tennyson ... 895

The Jewels
Guy de Maupassant ... 975

Once upon a Time
Nadine Gordimer ... 1141

Araby
James Joyce ... 1174

Axolotl
Julio Cortázar ... 1217

The Book of Sand
Jorge Luis Borges ... 1225

Half a Day
Naguib Mahfouz ... 1241

Like the Sun
R. K. Narayan ... 1282

GOOD VERSUS EVIL

from **The Pardoner's Tale**
Geoffrey Chaucer ... 167

Edward, Edward ... 226

The Fall of Satan *from* **Paradise Lost**
John Milton ... 401

The Tragedy of Macbeth
William Shakespeare ... 438

My Last Duchess
Robert Browning ... 908

The Mark of the Beast
Rudyard Kipling ... 931

Porphyria's Lover
Robert Browning ... 990

On the Bottom *from* **Survival in Auschwitz**
Primo Levi ... 1052

Never Shall I Forget
Elie Wiesel ... 1062

In the Shadow of War
Ben Okri ... 1093

The Second Coming
William Butler Yeats ... 1163

HEROES AND ANTIHEROES

from **Beowulf** ... 20

from **Gilgamesh: A Verse Narrative** ... 57

the **Iliad,** *from* **Book 22: The Death of Hector**
Homer ... 66

from **The Day of Destiny**
from **Le Morte d'Arthur**
Sir Thomas Malory ... 215

from **Sir Gawain and the Green Knight** ... 229

The Fall of Satan *from* **Paradise Lost**
John Milton ... 401

The Tragedy of Macbeth
William Shakespeare ... 438

Ulysses
Alfred, Lord Tennyson ... 903

My Last Duchess
Robert Browning ... 908

Dulce et Decorum Est
Wilfred Owen ... 1039

The Hollow Men
T. S. Eliot 1044

On the Bottom *from* **Survival in Auschwitz**
Primo Levi 1052

The Destructors
Graham Greene 1080

I am not one of those who left the land
Anna Akhmatova 1203

HUMOR AND THE STING OF SATIRE

Get Up and Bar the Door 132

Sonnet 130
William Shakespeare 320

A Modest Proposal
Jonathan Swift 580

from **The Rape of the Lock**
Alexander Pope 603

from **Candide**
Voltaire 618

from **Don Quixote**
Miguel de Cervantes 626

from **Gulliver's Travels**
Jonathan Swift
from **Part 1: A Voyage to Lilliput** 653
from **Part 2: A Voyage to Brobdingnag** .. 660

To a Louse
Robert Burns 843

Telephone Conversation
Wole Soyinka 1156

That's All
Harold Pinter 1339

THE INDIVIDUAL AND SOCIETY

from **A History of the English Church and People**
Bede 84

The Prologue *from* **The Canterbury Tales**
Geoffrey Chaucer 140

Blow, Blow, Thou Winter Wind
William Shakespeare 322

Meditation 17
John Donne 343

Tilbury Speech
Queen Elizabeth I 366

from **Don Quixote**
Miguel de Cervantes 626

from **The Education of Women**
Daniel Defoe 647

from **The Life of Samuel Johnson**
James Boswell 670

Tanka 751

Question and Answer Among the Mountains
Li Po 821

The Mark of the Beast
Rudyard Kipling 931

The Bet
Anton Chekhov 966

Shakespeare's Sister
from **A Room of One's Own**
Virginia Woolf 1105

Shooting an Elephant
George Orwell 1116

No Witchcraft for Sale
Doris Lessing 1126

I am not one of those who left the land
Anna Akhmatova 1203

The Book of Sand
Jorge Luis Borges 1225

Digging
Seamus Heaney 1246

The Doll's House
Katherine Mansfield 1253

Musée des Beaux Arts
W. H. Auden 1264

Games at Twilight
Anita Desai 1289

The Soldier
Rupert Brooke 1330

Not Waving but Drowning
Stevie Smith 1337

That's All
Harold Pinter 1339

INNOCENCE AND EXPERIENCE

The Fall of Satan *from* **Paradise Lost**
John Milton 401

from **Candide**
Voltaire 618

The Tyger
William Blake 720

The Lamb
William Blake 723

The Chimney Sweeper
from **Songs of Innocence**
William Blake 725

The Chimney Sweeper
from **Songs of Experience**
William Blake 727

A Poison Tree
William Blake 731

The Silver Fifty-Sen Pieces
Yasunari Kawabata 1072

In the Shadow of War
Ben Okri 1093

Araby
James Joyce 1174

The Rocking-Horse Winner
D. H. Lawrence 1186

The Doll's House
Katherine Mansfield 1253

Fern Hill
Dylan Thomas 1271

Games at Twilight
Anita Desai 1289

Next Term, We'll Mash You
Penelope Lively 1299

LOSS AND DEATH

from **Gilgamesh: A Verse Narrative** 57

The Wife's Lament 92

from **The Pardoner's Tale**
Geoffrey Chaucer 167

Sonnet 71
William Shakespeare 317

Fear No More the Heat o' the Sun
William Shakespeare 324

To be, or not to be *from* **Hamlet**
William Shakespeare 328

Tomorrow, and tomorrow, and tomorrow
from **The Tragedy of Macbeth**
William Shakespeare 331

Meditation 17
John Donne 343

Death be not proud
John Donne 348

On My First Son
Ben Jonson 354

When I consider how my light is spent
John Milton 415

from **A Journal of the Plague Year**
Daniel Defoe 663

Elegy Written in a Country Churchyard
Thomas Gray 676

When I Have Fears
John Keats 827

Ulysses
Alfred, Lord Tennyson 903

To an Athlete Dying Young
A. E. Housman 926

from **In Memoriam A.H.H.**
Alfred, Lord Tennyson 984

Crossing the Bar
Alfred, Lord Tennyson 989

Ah, Are You Digging on My Grave?
Thomas Hardy 996

Never Shall I Forget
Elie Wiesel 1062

Lot's Wife
Anna Akhmatova 1201

All the unburied ones
Anna Akhmatova 1203

Do Not Go Gentle into That Good Night
Dylan Thomas 1274

LOVE'S SORROWS, LOVE'S TRIUMPHS

Lord Randall 130

from **The Wife of Bath's Tale**
Geoffrey Chaucer 177

Federigo's Falcon *from the* **Decameron**
Giovanni Boccaccio 208

The Passionate Shepherd to His Love
Christopher Marlowe 293

The Nymph's Reply to the Shepherd
Sir Walter Raleigh 297

To the Virgins, to Make Much of Time
Robert Herrick 299

To His Coy Mistress
Andrew Marvell 303

Sonnet 29
William Shakespeare 314

Sonnet 30
William Shakespeare 316

Sonnet 71
William Shakespeare 317

Sonnet 73
William Shakespeare 318

Sonnet 116
William Shakespeare 319

Sonnet 130
William Shakespeare 320

Sonnet 23
Louise Labé 321

Song
John Donne 337

A Valediction: Forbidding Mourning
John Donne 340

On My First Son
Ben Jonson 354

Song: To Celia
Ben Jonson 356

Whoso List to Hunt
Sir Thomas Wyatt 530

Sonnet 30
Edmund Spenser 532

Sonnet 75
Edmund Spenser 534

Why So Pale and Wan, Fond Lover?
Sir John Suckling 535

To Lucasta, on Going to the Wars
Richard Lovelace 537

To Althea, from Prison
Richard Lovelace 538

Letter to His Two Small Children
Li Po 822

Sonnet 43
Elizabeth Barrett Browning 914

Dover Beach
Matthew Arnold 921

When I Was One-and-Twenty
A. E. Housman 998

The Demon Lover
Elizabeth Bowen 1206

Fear
Gabriela Mistral 1267

Sonnet 79 / Soneto 79
Pablo Neruda 1278

OPPRESSION AND FREEDOM

from **The Wife of Bath's Tale**
Geoffrey Chaucer 177

from **Female Orations**
Margaret Cavendish, duchess of Newcastle 368

Psalm 137 376

from **A Vindication of the Rights of Woman**
Mary Wollstonecraft 637

To the Ladies
Mary, Lady Chudleigh 646

from **The Education of Women**
Daniel Defoe 647

Shakespeare's Sister
from **A Room of One's Own**
Virginia Woolf 1105

"The Noble Mansion of Free India"
Jawaharlal Nehru 1137

Marriage Is a Private Affair
Chinua Achebe 1148

Saboteur
Ha Jin 1308

from the **Universal Declaration of Human Rights**
United Nations Commission on Human Rights . 1318

from **The Question of South Africa**
Desmond Tutu 1320

from **Towards a True Refuge**
Aung San Suu Kyi 1324

PEOPLE AND NATURE

The Seafarer 87

Lines Composed a Few Miles Above Tintern Abbey
William Wordsworth 735

Tanka 751

Haiku 755

from **Childe Harold's Pilgrimage, Canto IV**
George Gordon, Lord Byron 796

Ode to the West Wind
Percy Bysshe Shelley 805

Night Thoughts Afloat
Tu Fu 817

Quiet Night Thoughts
Li Po 820

Question and Answer Among the Mountains
Li Po 821

Ode to a Nightingale
John Keats 830

To a Mouse
Robert Burns 840

from **Ode: Intimations of Immortality**
William Wordsworth 846

To a Skylark
Percy Bysshe Shelley 849

Pied Beauty
Gerard Manley Hopkins 917

The Darkling Thrush
Thomas Hardy 993

The Lake Isle of Innisfree
William Butler Yeats 1166

The Wild Swans at Coole
William Butler Yeats 1169

The Horses
Ted Hughes 1334

POWER AND AMBITION

from **Gilgamesh: A Verse Narrative** 57

The Tragedy of Macbeth
William Shakespeare 438

Ozymandias
Percy Bysshe Shelley 802

Jade Flower Palace
Tu Fu 815

How Much Land Does a Man Need?
Leo Tolstoy 950

"I Believe in a British Empire"
Joseph Chamberlain 1134

The Rocking-Horse Winner
D. H. Lawrence 1186

THE QUEST AND THE PERILOUS JOURNEY

from **Beowulf** 20

from **Gilgamesh: A Verse Narrative** 57

The Seafarer 87

from **The Third Voyage of Sindbad the Sailor**
from **The Thousand and One Nights** 201

from **The Day of Destiny**
from **Le Morte d'Arthur**
Sir Thomas Malory 215

from **Sir Gawain and the Green Knight** ... 229

from **The Pilgrim's Progress**
John Bunyan 419

from **Don Quixote**
Miguel de Cervantes 626

The Rime of the Ancient Mariner
Samuel Taylor Coleridge 762

Ulysses
Alfred, Lord Tennyson 903

Araby
James Joyce 1174

The Rocking-Horse Winner
D. H. Lawrence 1186

THE SEARCH FOR WISDOM

Right-Mind and Wrong-Mind
from the **Panchatantra** 194

Of Studies
Francis Bacon 360

Psalm 23 374

The Parable of the Prodigal Son 378

Night *from the* **Koran** 385

from **Philosophy and Spiritual Discipline**
from the **Bhagavad-Gita** 387

Zen Parables 389

from **The Analects of Confucius** 391

from the **Tao Te Ching**
Lao Tzu 392

Taoist Anecdotes 393

Sayings of Saadi
Saadi 394

African Proverbs 395

When I consider how my light is spent
John Milton 415

from **The Pilgrim's Progress**
John Bunyan 419

Heroic Couplets
Alexander Pope 598

from **An Essay on Man**
Alexander Pope 601

The Bet
Anton Chekhov 966

THE TRANSFORMING IMAGINATION

Full Fathom Five
William Shakespeare 326

Lines Composed a Few Miles Above Tintern Abbey
William Wordsworth 735

Composed upon Westminster Bridge
William Wordsworth 743

Kubla Khan
Samuel Taylor Coleridge 758

She Walks in Beauty
George Gordon, Lord Byron 794

from **Childe Harold's Pilgrimage, Canto IV**
George Gordon, Lord Byron 796

Ode to the West Wind
Percy Bysshe Shelley 805

Quiet Night Thoughts
Li Po 820

On First Looking into Chapman's Homer
John Keats 825

Ode to a Nightingale
John Keats 830

Ode on a Grecian Urn
John Keats 835

The Lake Isle of Innisfree
William Butler Yeats 1166

The Rocking-Horse Winner
D. H. Lawrence 1186

The Demon Lover
Elizabeth Bowen 1206

Axolotl
Julio Cortázar 1217

The Book of Sand
Jorge Luis Borges 1225

B. Wordsworth
V. S. Naipaul 1233

Fern Hill
Dylan Thomas 1271

Sailing to Byzantium
William Butler Yeats 1332

THE WAGES OF WAR

the **Iliad,** *from* **Book 22: The Death of Hector**
Homer 66

Saint Crispin's Day Speech *from* **Henry V**
William Shakespeare 332

Tilbury Speech
Queen Elizabeth I 366

Dulce et Decorum Est
Wilfred Owen 1039

The Hollow Men
T. S. Eliot 1044

On the Bottom *from* **Survival in Auschwitz**
Primo Levi 1052

from **The War**
Marguerite Duras 1058

Blood, Sweat, and Tears
Winston Churchill 1067

The Silver Fifty-Sen Pieces
Yasunari Kawabata 1072

The Destructors
Graham Greene 1080

In the Shadow of War
Ben Okri 1093

The Second Coming
William Butler Yeats 1163

SELECTIONS BY GENRE

FICTION

ALLEGORY

from **The Pilgrim's Progress**
John Bunyan 419

ANECDOTES

Taoist Anecdotes 393

DEBATE

from **Female Orations**
Margaret Cavendish, duchess of Newcastle 368

FABLE

Right-Mind and Wrong-Mind
from the Panchatantra 194

NOVEL EXCERPTS

from **Grendel**
John Gardner 39

from **Candide**
Voltaire 618

from **Don Quixote**
Miguel de Cervantes 626

from **Gulliver's Travels**
Jonathan Swift

from **Part 1: A Voyage to Lilliput** 653

from **Part 2: A Voyage to Brobdingnag** 660

from **A Journal of the Plague Year**
Daniel Defoe 663

PARABLES

The Parable of the Prodigal Son 378

Zen Parables 389

PARODY

Macbeth and the Witches
Richard Armour 524

ROMANCE NARRATIVE

from **The Day of Destiny**
from **Le Morte d'Arthur**
Sir Thomas Malory 215

from **Sir Gawain and the Green Knight** 229

TALES / SHORT STORIES

from **The Third Voyage of Sindbad the Sailor**
from **The Thousand and One Nights** 201

Federigo's Falcon *from the* **Decameron**
Giovanni Boccaccio 208

Top of the Food Chain
T. Coraghessan Boyle 590

The Mark of the Beast
Rudyard Kipling 931

How Much Land Does a Man Need?
Leo Tolstoy 950

The Bet
Anton Chekhov 966

The Jewels
Guy de Maupassant 975

The Silver Fifty-Sen Pieces
Yasunari Kawabata 1072

The Destructors
Graham Greene 1080

In the Shadow of War
Ben Okri 1093

No Witchcraft for Sale
Doris Lessing 1126

Once upon a Time
Nadine Gordimer 1141

Marriage Is a Private Affair
Chinua Achebe 1148

Araby
James Joyce 1174

The Rocking-Horse Winner
D. H. Lawrence 1186

The Demon Lover
Elizabeth Bowen 1206

Axolotl
Julio Cortázar 1217

The Book of Sand
Jorge Luis Borges 1225

B. Wordsworth
V. S. Naipaul 1233

Half a Day
Naguib Mahfouz 1241

The Doll's House
Katherine Mansfield 1253

Like the Sun
R. K. Narayan 1282

Games at Twilight
Anita Desai 1289

Next Term, We'll Mash You
Penelope Lively 1299

Saboteur
Ha Jin 1308

DRAMA

The Tragedy of Macbeth
William Shakespeare 438

That's All
Harold Pinter 1339

DRAMATIC EXCERPTS

To be, or not to be *from* **Hamlet**
William Shakespeare 328

Tomorrow, and tomorrow, and tomorrow
from **The Tragedy of Macbeth**
William Shakespeare 331

Saint Crispin's Day Speech *from* **Henry V**
William Shakespeare 332

Our revels now are ended *from* **The Tempest**
William Shakespeare 334

from **W;t**
Margaret Edson 350

POETRY

BALLADS

Lord Randall 130

Get Up and Bar the Door 132

Edward, Edward 226

The Twa Corbies 262

Raven doth to raven fly
Alexander Pushkin 263

DRAMATIC MONOLOGUE

My Last Duchess
Robert Browning 908

Porphyria's Lover
Robert Browning 990

ELEGY

Elegy Written in a Country Churchyard
Thomas Gray 676

from **In Memoriam A.H.H.**
Alfred, Lord Tennyson 984

EPICS

from **Beowulf**
The Monster Grendel 21
The Arrival of the Hero 24
Unferth's Challenge 26
The Battle with Grendel 31
The Monster's Mother 36
The Final Battle 43

from **Gilgamesh: A Verse Narrative** 57

the **Iliad,** *from* **Book 22: The Death of Hector**
Homer 66

The Fall of Satan *from* **Paradise Lost**
John Milton 401

HAIKU

Haiku 755

LYRICS

Break, Break, Break
Alfred, Lord Tennyson 106

The Passionate Shepherd to His Love
Christopher Marlowe 293

The Nymph's Reply to the Shepherd
Sir Walter Raleigh 297

To the Virgins, to Make Much of Time
Robert Herrick 299

To His Coy Mistress
Andrew Marvell 303

Song
John Donne 337

A Valediction: Forbidding Mourning
John Donne 340

On My First Son
Ben Jonson 354

Song: To Celia
Ben Jonson 356

Why So Pale and Wan, Fond Lover?
Sir John Suckling 535

To Lucasta, on Going to the Wars
Richard Lovelace 537

To Althea, from Prison
Richard Lovelace 538

When You Are Old
Pierre de Ronsard 552

When You Are Old
William Butler Yeats 553

To the Ladies
Mary, Lady Chudleigh 646

The Tyger
William Blake 720

The Lamb
William Blake 723

The Chimney Sweeper
from **Songs of Innocence**
William Blake 725

The Chimney Sweeper
from **Songs of Experience**
William Blake 727

A Poison Tree
William Blake 731

Lines Composed a Few Miles Above Tintern Abbey
William Wordsworth 735

Kubla Khan
Samuel Taylor Coleridge 758

She Walks in Beauty
George Gordon, Lord Byron 794

SELECTIONS BY GENRE

Jade Flower Palace
Tu Fu 815

Night Thoughts Afloat
Tu Fu 817

Quiet Night Thoughts
Li Po 820

Question and Answer Among the Mountains
Li Po 821

Letter to His Two Small Children
Li Po 822

To a Mouse
Robert Burns 840

To a Louse
Robert Burns 843

To a Skylark
Percy Bysshe Shelley 849

London
William Blake 866

The Virgins
Derek Walcott 867

Ulysses
Alfred, Lord Tennyson 903

Pied Beauty
Gerard Manley Hopkins 917

Dover Beach
Matthew Arnold 921

To an Athlete Dying Young
A. E. Housman 926

Crossing the Bar
Alfred, Lord Tennyson 989

The Darkling Thrush
Thomas Hardy 993

Ah, Are You Digging on My Grave?
Thomas Hardy 996

When I Was One-and-Twenty
A. E. Housman 998

Drummer Hodge
Thomas Hardy 1010

The Sleeper of the Valley
Arthur Rimbaud 1011

Dulce et Decorum Est
Wilfred Owen 1039

The Rear-Guard
Siegfried Sassoon 1041

The Hollow Men
T. S. Eliot 1044

Never Shall I Forget
Elie Wiesel 1062

The End and the Beginning
Wisława Szymborska 1098

Telephone Conversation
Wole Soyinka 1156

The Second Coming
William Butler Yeats 1163

The Lake Isle of Innisfree
William Butler Yeats 1166

The Wild Swans at Coole
William Butler Yeats 1169

The Swan
Rainer Maria Rilke 1171

Lot's Wife
Anna Akhmatova 1201

All the unburied ones
Anna Akhmatova 1203

I am not one of those who left the land
Anna Akhmatova 1203

Digging
Seamus Heaney 1246

Musée des Beaux Arts
W. H. Auden 1264

Fear
Gabriela Mistral 1267

Fern Hill
Dylan Thomas 1271

Do Not Go Gentle into That Good Night
Dylan Thomas 1274

Sailing to Byzantium
William Butler Yeats 1332

The Horses
Ted Hughes 1334

Not Waving but Drowning
Stevie Smith 1337

The Lorelei
Heinrich Heine 1356

Siren Song
Margaret Atwood 1357

MOCK EPIC

from **The Rape of the Lock**
Alexander Pope 603

NARRATIVE POETRY

The Seafarer 87

The Wife's Lament 92

from **The Wanderer** 104

from **The Canterbury Tales**
Geoffrey Chaucer
The Prologue 140
from **The Pardoner's Tale** 167
from **The Wife of Bath's Tale** 177

The Rime of the Ancient Mariner
Samuel Taylor Coleridge 762

from **Childe Harold's Pilgrimage, Canto IV**
George Gordon, Lord Byron 796

The Lady of Shalott
Alfred, Lord Tennyson 895

ODES

Ode to the West Wind
Percy Bysshe Shelley 805

Ode to a Nightingale
John Keats 830

Ode on a Grecian Urn
John Keats 835

from **Ode: Intimations of Immortality**
William Wordsworth 846

PHILOSOPHICAL VERSE

Heroic Couplets
Alexander Pope 598

from **An Essay on Man**
Alexander Pope 601

PSALMS

Psalm 23 374

Psalm 137 376

SONGS

Blow, Blow, Thou Winter Wind
William Shakespeare 322

Fear No More the Heat o' the Sun
William Shakespeare 324

Full Fathom Five
William Shakespeare 326

SONNETS

Sonnet 42
Francesco Petrarch 312

Sonnet 18
William Shakespeare 313

Sonnet 29
William Shakespeare 314

Sonnet 30
William Shakespeare 316

Sonnet 71
William Shakespeare 317

Sonnet 73
William Shakespeare 318

Sonnet 116
William Shakespeare 319

Sonnet 130
William Shakespeare 320

Sonnet 23
Louise Labé 321

Death be not proud
John Donne 348

When I consider how my light is spent
John Milton 415

Whoso List to Hunt
Sir Thomas Wyatt 530

Sonnet 30
Edmund Spenser 532

Sonnet 75
Edmund Spenser 534

Composed upon Westminster Bridge
William Wordsworth 743

The World Is Too Much with Us
William Wordsworth 745

Ozymandias
Percy Bysshe Shelley 802

On First Looking into Chapman's Homer
John Keats 825

When I Have Fears
John Keats 827

Sonnet 43
Elizabeth Barrett Browning 914

Sonnet 79 / Soneto 79
Pablo Neruda 1278

The Soldier
Rupert Brooke 1330

TANKA

Tanka 751

NONFICTION AND INFORMATIONAL TEXT

AXIOMS AND MAXIMS

Axioms *from the* **Essays**
Francis Bacon 363

from **The Analects of Confucius** 391

Sayings of Saadi
Saadi 394

BIOGRAPHY

from **The Life of Samuel Johnson**
James Boswell 670

CRITICAL COMMENTS

Macbeth's Porter 470

The King's Evil 505

Hecate: Queen of the Night 506

Soliloquies and Asides 521

The Mystery of Evil 522

Shelley and the Ode 809

Dialogue with the Soul 834

The Arc of Experience 838

Escaping a World of Shadows 901

Love Is Itself a Faith 923

The Influence of James Joyce 1180

CULTURAL COMMENTARY

Women in Anglo-Saxon Culture 12

"A Terrible Worm in an Iron Cocoon" 120

Money, Gunpowder, and the Middle Class: The End of an Era 126

Places of Pilgrimage 150

The Archetype of Arthur 220

The Glass of Fashion 291

The Bard and the Database 478

Life Among the Haves 568

. . . and Life Among the Have-Nots 570

The Lure of the Gothic 714

An Irresistible Bad Boy: The Byronic Hero 799

An Age in Need of Heroines: Reform in Victorian Britain 882

The Pre-Raphaelite Brotherhood: Challenging Artistic Authority 884

Victorian Drama: From Relief to Realism 890

The Age of Empire 936

Votes for Women! 1111

DEFINITIONS

from **A Dictionary of the English Language**
Samuel Johnson 667

DIARY

from **The Diary of Samuel Pepys**
Samuel Pepys 695

ESSAYS

Of Studies
Francis Bacon 360

from **On the Knocking at the Gate in *Macbeth***
Thomas De Quincey 468

A Modest Proposal
Jonathan Swift 580

from **The Education of Women**
Daniel Defoe 647

Shakespeare's Sister
from **A Room of One's Own**
Virginia Woolf 1105

Shooting an Elephant
George Orwell 1116

HISTORIES

The Fury of the Northmen
Ellen Ashdown 49

Trojan Gold *from* **Gods, Graves, and Scholars**
C. W. Ceram 77

from **A History of the English Church and People**
Bede 84

Give Us This Day Our Daily Bread
Joseph Papp *and* Elizabeth Kirkland 305

from **The Burning of Rome** *from* **The Annals**
Tacitus 694

Death and Other Grave Matters
Daniel Pool 928

LETTERS

"Blake Is a Real Name . . ."
Charles Lamb 722

Coleridge Describes His Addiction
Samuel Taylor Coleridge 787

Keats's Last Letter
John Keats 829

D. H. Lawrence on Money
D. H. Lawrence 1198

MAGAZINE AND NEWSPAPER ARTICLES

Life in 999: A Grim Struggle
Howard G. Chua-Eoan 40

Scenes from a Modern Marriage
Julia Markus 911

MEDITATION

Meditation 17
John Donne 343

MEMOIRS

On the Bottom *from* **Survival in Auschwitz**
Primo Levi 1052

from **The War**
Marguerite Duras 1058

PROVERBS

African Proverbs 395

SACRED TEXTS

Night *from the* **Koran** 385

from **Philosophy and Spiritual Discipline**
from the **Bhagavad-Gita** 387

from the **Tao Te Ching**
Lao Tzu 392

TRAVEL BOOK

from **In Patagonia**
Bruce Chatwin 788

WEB PAGE

Kristallnacht Web page *from* **The United States Holocaust Memorial Museum** 1064

PUBLIC DOCUMENTS

DEBATE

from **Female Orations**
Margaret Cavendish, duchess of Newcastle 368

PLATFORM

from **A Vindication of the Rights of Woman**
Mary Wollstonecraft 637

POLITICAL STATEMENT

from the **Universal Declaration of Human Rights**
United Nations Commission on Human Rights 1318

SPEECHES

Tilbury Speech
Queen Elizabeth I 366

Blood, Sweat, and Tears
Winston Churchill 1067

"I Believe in a British Empire"
Joseph Chamberlain 1134

"The Noble Mansion of Free India"
Jawaharlal Nehru 1137

from **The Question of South Africa**
Desmond Tutu 1320

from **Towards a True Refuge**
Aung San Suu Kyi 1324

TESTIMONY

from **Evidence Given Before the Sadler Committee**
Peter Smart 728

SELECTIONS BY REGION

AFRICA

African Proverbs 395

In the Shadow of War
Ben Okri 1093

No Witchcraft for Sale
Doris Lessing 1126

Once upon a Time
Nadine Gordimer 1141

Marriage Is a Private Affair
Chinua Achebe 1148

Telephone Conversation
Wole Soyinka 1156

Half a Day
Naguib Mahfouz 1241

from **The Question of South Africa**
Desmond Tutu 1320

ASIA

from **Gilgamesh: A Verse Narrative** 57

Right-Mind and Wrong-Mind
from the **Panchatantra** 194

from **The Third Voyage of Sindbad the Sailor**
from **The Thousand and One Nights** 201

Night *from the* **Koran** 385

from **Philosophy and Spiritual Discipline**
from the **Bhagavad-Gita** 387

Zen Parables 389

from **The Analects of Confucius** 391

from the **Tao Te Ching**
Lao Tzu 392

Taoist Anecdotes 393

Sayings of Saadi
Saadi 394

Tanka 751

Haiku 755

Jade Flower Palace
Tu Fu 815

Night Thoughts Afloat
Tu Fu 817

Quiet Night Thoughts
Li Po 820

Question and Answer Among the Mountains
Li Po 821

Letter to His Two Small Children
Li Po 822

The Silver Fifty-Sen Pieces
Yasunari Kawabata 1072

"The Noble Mansion of Free India"
Jawaharlal Nehru 1137

Like the Sun
R. K. Narayan 1282

Games at Twilight
Anita Desai 1289

Saboteur
Ha Jin 1308

from **Towards a True Refuge**
Aung San Suu Kyi 1324

EUROPE

the **Iliad,** *from* **Book 22: The Death of Hector**
Homer 66

Federigo's Falcon *from the* **Decameron**
Giovanni Boccaccio 208

Raven doth to raven fly
Alexander Pushkin 263

Sonnet 42
Francesco Petrarch 312

Sonnet 23
Louise Labé 321

When You Are Old
Pierre de Ronsard 552

When You Are Old
William Butler Yeats 553

A Modest Proposal
Jonathan Swift 580

from **Candide**
Voltaire 618

from **Don Quixote**
Miguel de Cervantes 626

from **The Burning of Rome** *from* **The Annals**
Tacitus 694

How Much Land Does a Man Need?
Leo Tolstoy 950

The Bet
Anton Chekhov 966

The Jewels
Guy de Maupassant 975

The Sleeper of the Valley
Arthur Rimbaud 1011

On the Bottom *from* **Survival in Auschwitz**
Primo Levi 1052

from **The War**
Marguerite Duras 1058

Never Shall I Forget
Elie Wiesel 1062

The End and the Beginning
Wisława Szymborska 1098

The Second Coming
William Butler Yeats 1163

The Lake Isle of Innisfree
William Butler Yeats 1166

The Wild Swans at Coole
William Butler Yeats 1169

The Swan
Rainer Maria Rilke 1171

Araby
James Joyce 1174

Lot's Wife
Anna Akhmatova 1201

All the unburied ones
Anna Akhmatova 1203

I am not one of those who left the land
Anna Akhmatova 1203

The Demon Lover
Elizabeth Bowen 1206

Digging
Seamus Heaney 1246

The Lorelei
Heinrich Heine 1356

GREAT BRITAIN

from **Beowulf** 20

from **A History of the English Church and People**
Bede 84

The Seafarer 87

The Wife's Lament 92

from **The Wanderer** 104

Break, Break, Break
Alfred, Lord Tennyson 106

The Prologue *from* **The Canterbury Tales**
Geoffrey Chaucer 140

from **The Pardoner's Tale**
Geoffrey Chaucer 167

from **The Wife of Bath's Tale**
Geoffrey Chaucer 177

from **The Day of Destiny**
from **Le Morte d'Arthur**
Sir Thomas Malory 215

Edward, Edward 226

from **Sir Gawain and the Green Knight** 229

The Twa Corbies 262

The Passionate Shepherd to His Love
Christopher Marlowe 293

The Nymph's Reply to the Shepherd
Sir Walter Raleigh 297

To the Virgins, to Make Much of Time
Robert Herrick 299

To His Coy Mistress
Andrew Marvell 303

Sonnet 18
William Shakespeare 313

Sonnet 29
William Shakespeare 314

Sonnet 30
William Shakespeare 316

Sonnet 71
William Shakespeare 317

Sonnet 73
William Shakespeare 318

Sonnet 116
William Shakespeare 319

Sonnet 130
William Shakespeare 320

Blow, Blow, Thou Winter Wind
William Shakespeare 322

Fear No More the Heat o' the Sun
William Shakespeare 324

Full Fathom Five
William Shakespeare 326

To be, or not to be *from* **Hamlet**
William Shakespeare 328

Tomorrow, and tomorrow, and tomorrow
from **The Tragedy of Macbeth**
William Shakespeare 331

Saint Crispin's Day Speech *from* **Henry V**
William Shakespeare 332

Our revels now are ended
from **The Tempest**
William Shakespeare 334

Song
John Donne 337

A Valediction: Forbidding Mourning
John Donne 340

Meditation 17
John Donne 343

Death be not proud
John Donne 348

On My First Son
Ben Jonson 354

Song: To Celia
Ben Jonson 356

Of Studies
Francis Bacon 360

Tilbury Speech
Queen Elizabeth I 366

from **Female Orations**
Margaret Cavendish, duchess of Newcastle 368

Psalm 23 374

Psalm 137 376

The Parable of the Prodigal Son 378

The Fall of Satan *from* **Paradise Lost**
John Milton 401

When I consider how my light is spent
John Milton 415

from **The Pilgrim's Progress**
John Bunyan 419

The Tragedy of Macbeth
William Shakespeare 438

SELECTIONS BY REGION

from **On the Knocking at the Gate in *Macbeth***
Thomas De Quincey 468

Whoso List to Hunt
Sir Thomas Wyatt 530

Sonnet 30
Edmund Spenser 532

Sonnet 75
Edmund Spenser 534

Why So Pale and Wan, Fond Lover?
Sir John Suckling 535

To Lucasta, on Going to the Wars
Richard Lovelace 537

To Althea, from Prison
Richard Lovelace 538

Heroic Couplets
Alexander Pope 598

from **An Essay on Man**
Alexander Pope 601

from **The Rape of the Lock**
Alexander Pope 603

from **A Vindication of the Rights of Woman**
Mary Wollstonecraft 637

To the Ladies
Mary, Lady Chudleigh 646

from **The Education of Women**
Daniel Defoe 647

from **Gulliver's Travels**
Jonathan Swift
- *from* **Part 1: A Voyage to Lilliput** 653
- *from* **Part 2: A Voyage to Brobdingnag** .. 660

from **A Journal of the Plague Year**
Daniel Defoe 663

from **A Dictionary of the English Language**
Samuel Johnson 667

from **The Life of Samuel Johnson**
James Boswell 670

Elegy Written in a Country Churchyard
Thomas Gray 676

from **The Diary of Samuel Pepys**
Samuel Pepys 695

The Tyger
William Blake 720

"Blake Is a Real Name . . ."
Charles Lamb 722

The Lamb
William Blake 723

The Chimney Sweeper
from **Songs of Innocence**
William Blake 725

The Chimney Sweeper
from **Songs of Experience**
William Blake 727

from **Evidence Given Before the Sadler Committee**
Peter Smart 728

A Poison Tree
William Blake 731

Lines Composed a Few Miles Above Tintern Abbey
William Wordsworth 735

Composed upon Westminster Bridge
William Wordsworth 743

The World Is Too Much with Us
William Wordsworth 745

Kubla Khan
Samuel Taylor Coleridge 758

The Rime of the Ancient Mariner
Samuel Taylor Coleridge 762

Coleridge Describes His Addiction
Samuel Taylor Coleridge 787

from **In Patagonia**
Bruce Chatwin 788

She Walks in Beauty
George Gordon, Lord Byron 794

from **Childe Harold's Pilgrimage, Canto IV**
George Gordon, Lord Byron 796

Ozymandias
Percy Bysshe Shelley 802

Ode to the West Wind
Percy Bysshe Shelley 805

On First Looking into Chapman's Homer
John Keats 825

When I Have Fears
John Keats 827

Keats's Last Letter
John Keats 829

Ode to a Nightingale
John Keats 830

Ode on a Grecian Urn
John Keats 835

To a Mouse
Robert Burns 840

To a Louse
Robert Burns 843

from **Ode: Intimations of Immortality**
William Wordsworth 846

To a Skylark
Percy Bysshe Shelley 849

London
William Blake 866

The Lady of Shalott
Alfred, Lord Tennyson 895

Ulysses
Alfred, Lord Tennyson 903

My Last Duchess
Robert Browning 908

Sonnet 43
Elizabeth Barrett Browning 914

Pied Beauty
Gerard Manley Hopkins 917

Dover Beach
Matthew Arnold 921

To an Athlete Dying Young
A. E. Housman 926

The Mark of the Beast
Rudyard Kipling 931

from **In Memoriam A.H.H.**
Alfred, Lord Tennyson 984

Crossing the Bar
Alfred, Lord Tennyson 989

Porphyria's Lover
Robert Browning 990

The Darkling Thrush
Thomas Hardy 993

Ah, Are You Digging on My Grave?
Thomas Hardy 996

When I Was One-and-Twenty
A. E. Housman 998

Drummer Hodge
Thomas Hardy 1010

Dulce et Decorum Est
Wilfred Owen 1039

The Rear-Guard
Siegfried Sassoon 1041

The Hollow Men
T. S. Eliot 1044

Blood, Sweat, and Tears
Winston Churchill 1067

The Destructors
Graham Greene 1080

Shakespeare's Sister
from **A Room of One's Own**
Virginia Woolf 1105

Shooting an Elephant
George Orwell 1116

"I Believe in a British Empire"
Joseph Chamberlain 1134

The Rocking-Horse Winner
D. H. Lawrence 1186

D. H. Lawrence on Money
D. H. Lawrence 1198

Musée des Beaux Arts
W. H. Auden 1264

Fern Hill
Dylan Thomas 1271

Do Not Go Gentle into That Good Night
Dylan Thomas 1274

Next Term, We'll Mash You
Penelope Lively 1299

The Soldier
Rupert Brooke 1330

Sailing to Byzantium
William Butler Yeats 1332

The Horses
Ted Hughes 1334

Not Waving but Drowning
Stevie Smith 1337

That's All
Harold Pinter 1339

NORTH AMERICA

Life in 999: A Grim Struggle
Howard G. Chua-Eoan 40

The Fury of the Northmen
Ellen Ashdown 49

Trojan Gold *from* **Gods, Graves, and Scholars**
C. W. Ceram 77

Give Us This Day Our Daily Bread
Joseph Papp *and* Elizabeth Kirkland 305

from **W;t**
Margaret Edson 350

Macbeth and the Witches
Richard Armour 524

Top of the Food Chain
T. Coraghessan Boyle 590

Scenes from a Modern Marriage
Julia Markus 911

Death and Other Grave Matters
Daniel Pool 928

Siren Song
Margaret Atwood 1357

NEW ZEALAND

The Doll's House
Katherine Mansfield 1253

SOUTH AMERICA

Axolotl
Julio Cortázar 1217

The Book of Sand
Jorge Luis Borges 1225

Fear
Gabriela Mistral 1267

Sonnet 79 / Soneto 79
Pablo Neruda 1278

WEST INDIES

The Virgins
Derek Walcott 867

B. Wordsworth
V. S. Naipaul 1233

SKILLS, WORKSHOPS, AND FEATURES

SKILLS

LITERARY SKILLS

Epic Hero 20, 54
Alliteration 51, 758, 917, 1166, 1168
Kennings 51
Foil 57
Epic Simile 66
Epic Conventions 81
Ballad 130, 133
Character 140, 166
Frame Story 140, 191
Imagery 166, 751, 820, 1289
Irony 167, 208, 580, 802, 1116, 1148, 1183, 1282, 1308
Narrator 177
Couplets 189, 926
Fable 194
Archetype 201
Romance Hero 215
Pastoral 293
Carpe Diem 299
Sonnet 311, 314, 825, 914
Dramatic Song 322
Monologue and Soliloquy 328
Metaphysical Poetry 337, 339
Metaphysical Conceits 340
Tone 343, 637
Paradox 348, 1225
Epigram 354, 602
Parallelism 360, 374, 725
Parable 378
Didactic Literature 382, 385
Style 401, 412
Allusion 415, 745, 1044
Allegory 419, 950
Tragedy 438
Blank Verse 456, 735
Connotations 595
Antithesis 598
Mock Epic 603
Satire 614, 618, 1156
Parody 626
Symbol 720, 1141, 1169, 1186, 1253
Theme 731, 903, 966, 975, 1072, 1126, 1163, 1201, 1299
Personification 743
Romantic Lyric 747
Literary Ballad 762
Simile 794
Apostrophe 796, 810
Ode 805
Terza Rima 810
Mood 815, 921
Synesthesia 830
Metaphor 835, 1246, 1278
Word Music 895
Dramatic Monologue 908
Assonance 917, 1166, 1168

Conflict 931
Figures of Speech 1039
Memoir 1052
Setting 1080, 1233
Point of View 1093
Essay 1105
Epiphany 1174
Flashback 1206
Magic Realism 1217
Foreshadowing 1241
Modern Short Story 1261
Diction 1264
Refrain 1267
Lyric Poetry 1271
Elegy 1274
Villanelle 1276

READING SKILLS

Analyzing Style: Details 140
Interpreting Character 177
Evaluating Historical Context 208, 1052, 1126
Drawing Inferences 358, 908, 975, 1072
Analyzing Arguments 360, 647, 1045, 1067
Milton's Style 401
Recognizing Persuasive Techniques 580
Identifying the Writer's Stance 598
Analyzing Rhetorical Devices 635
Noting Patterns of Organization 637, 735
Reading Archaic Words 762
Reading Rhyme and Rhythm 796
Reading Inverted Syntax 825
Visualizing Imagery 835
Identifying Contrasting Images 895
Identifying Conflicts and Resolutions 931
Making Predictions 966, 1094, 1206, 1225
Comparing Main Ideas 1050, 1114, 1306
Implicit and Explicit Beliefs 1058, 1105
Inferring Motives 1080
Identifying the Author's Purpose 1116
Identifying Language Structures 1141
Comparing and Contrasting 1174
Identifying Point of View 1217
Analyzing Details 1289
Identifying Political Influences 1308

READING MATTERS

When the Text Is Tough 1363
Improving Your Comprehension 1364
Improving Your Reading Rate 1373
Vocabulary Development 1375

VOCABULARY SKILLS

Anglo-Saxon Legacy:
Words and Word Parts 53
Antonyms 166, 982, 1057, 1317
Distinguishing Multiple
Meanings of Words 190
Analogies 199, 596, 698, 791, 945, 1070, 1146, 1223, 1287, 1297
Semantic Mapping 206
Etymologies 213, 223, 613, 1124
Words Derived from Greek
and Latin Roots and Affixes 413
Context Clues 792, 1133, 1245, 1260
Synonyms 1057, 1317

WORKSHOPS

WRITING WORKSHOPS

Writing a Descriptive Essay 96
Reporting Literary Research 240
Analyzing Literature 542
Writing a Literary Essay 684
Writing a Reflective Essay 856
Comparing and Contrasting Literature 1002

MINI-WORKSHOPS

Writing a Persuasive Essay 1101
Analyzing Nonfiction 1159
Writing a Short Story 1249

LISTENING AND SPEAKING WORKSHOPS

Presenting Literary Research 260
Reciting Literature 550
Presenting a Literary Response 692
Presenting a Reflection 864
Presenting and Analyzing Speeches 1352

MEDIA WORKSHOP

Analyzing and Using Media 1344

FEATURES

A CLOSER LOOK

Women in Anglo-Saxon Culture 12
"A Terrible Worm in an Iron Cocoon" 120
Money, Gunpowder, and the Middle Class: The End of an Era 126
Places of Pilgrimage 150
The Archetype of Arthur 220
The Glass of Fashion 291
The Bard and the Database 478
Life Among the Haves 568
...and Life Among the Have-Nots 570
The Lure of the Gothic 714
An Irresistible Bad Boy: The Byronic Hero 799
An Age in Need of Heroines: Reform in Victorian Britain 882
The Pre-Raphaelite Brotherhood: Challenging Artistic Authority 884
Victorian Drama: From Relief to Realism 890
The Age of Empire 936
Votes for Women! 1111

COMPARING POINTS OF VIEW

Education and Equality 358
Women's Rights 634
The Holocaust 1050
Colonialism 1114
Human Rights 1306

CONNECTING TO WORLD LITERATURE

Epics: Stories on a Grand Scale *by* David Adams Leeming . . . 54

The Frame Story: A Tale Linking Tales *by* David Adams Leeming . . . 191

Worlds of Wisdom: Wisdom Literature . . . 382

The Sting of Satire *by* Robert DeMaria, Jr. . . . 614

Tanka and Haiku . . . 749

The Golden Age of Chinese Poetry . . . 811

The Rise of Realism . . . 946

CRITICAL COMMENTS

Macbeth's Porter . . . 470

The King's Evil . . . 505

Hecate: Queen of the Night . . . 506

Soliloquies and Asides . . . 521

The Mystery of Evil . . . 522

Shelley and the Ode . . . 809

Dialogue with the Soul . . . 834

The Arc of Experience . . . 838

Escaping a World of Shadows . . . 901

Love Is Itself a Faith . . . 923

The Influence of James Joyce . . . 1180

PRIMARY SOURCES

Axioms *from the* Essays Francis Bacon . . . 363

"Blake Is a Real Name . . ." Charles Lamb . . . 722

from Evidence Given Before the Sadler Committee Peter Smart . . . 728

Coleridge Describes His Addiction Samuel Taylor Coleridge . . . 787

Keats's Last Letter John Keats . . . 829

D. H. Lawrence on Money D. H. Lawrence . . . 1198

REFLECTING ON THE LITERARY PERIOD

The Anglo-Saxons: 449–1066 . . . 83

The Middle Ages: 1066–1485 . . . 225

The Renaissance: 1485–1660 . . . 529

The Restoration and the Eighteenth Century: 1660–1800 . . . 651

The Romantic Period: 1798–1832 . . . 839

The Victorian Period: 1832–1901 . . . 983

The Modern World: 1900 to the Present . . . 1329

GRAMMAR LINK

Make It Clear: Sentence Fragments and Run-on Sentences . . . 82

Linking It Up: Combining Sentences with Coordinating and Subordinating Conjunctions . . . 224

Appropriate Additions: Adjective Clauses and Adverb Clauses . . . 347

Make Sure It Agrees: Subject-Verb Agreement . . . 645

The Right Tense for Sense: Verb Tense Consistency . . . 733

Choosing the Right Reference: Pronoun and Antecedent Agreement . . . 964

Effective Sentences: The Power of Parallelism . . . 1078

The Wrong Place at the Wrong Time: Dangling Modifiers 1154

Building Coherence: Connecting Ideas 1215

Active-Voice Verbs and Passive-Voice Verbs 1262

LANGUAGE HANDBOOK

The Parts of Speech 1436

Agreement 1437

Using Verbs 1439

Using Pronouns 1441

Using Modifiers 1443

Phrases 1444

Clauses 1446

Sentence Structure 1447

Sentence Style 1450

Sentence Combining 1453

Capitalization 1454

Punctuation 1457, 1460

Spelling 1465

Glossary of Usage 1467

SKILLS REVIEW

Comparing Literature 104, 262, 552, 694, 866, 1010, 1356

Vocabulary 108, 266, 556, 698, 870, 1014, 1360

Writing 109, 267, 557, 699, 871, 1015, 1361

THE WORLD OF WORK

WRITER'S HANDBOOK

TEST SMARTS

Elements of Literature on the Internet

TO THE STUDENT

At the *Elements of Literature* Internet site, you can analyze the work of professional writers and learn the inside stories behind your favorite authors. You can also build your word power and analyze messages in the media. As you move through *Elements of Literature*, you will find the best online resources at **go.hrw.com.**

Here's how to log on:

1. Start your Web browser, and enter **go.hrw.com** in the Address or Location field.

2. Note the keyword in your textbook.

3. Enter the keyword, and click "go."

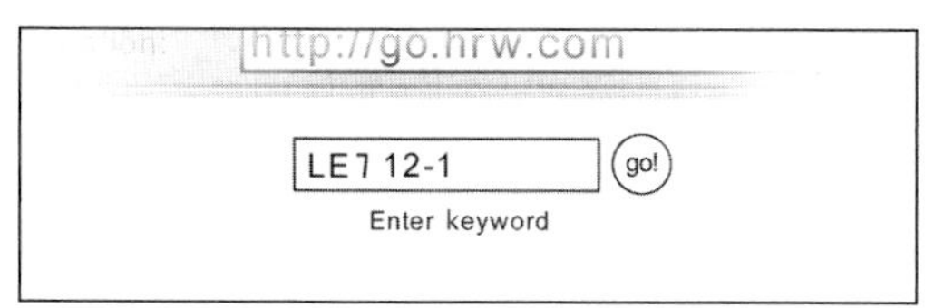

FEATURES OF THE SITE

More About the Writer
Author biographies provide the inside stories behind the lives and works of great writers.

More Writer's Models
Interactive Writer's Models present annotations and reading tips to help you with your own writing. Printable Professional Models and Student Models provide you with quality writing by real writers and students across the country.

Interactive Reading Model
Interactive Reading Workshops guide you through high-interest informational articles and allow you to share your opinions through pop-up questions and polls.

Vocabulary Practice
Interactive vocabulary-building activities help you build your word power.

Projects and Activities
Projects and activities help you extend your study of literature through writing, research, art, and public speaking.

Speeches
Video clips from historical speeches provide you with the tools you need to analyze elements of great speechmaking.

Media Tutorials
Media tutorials help you dissect messages in the media and learn to create your own multimedia presentations.

The British Isles

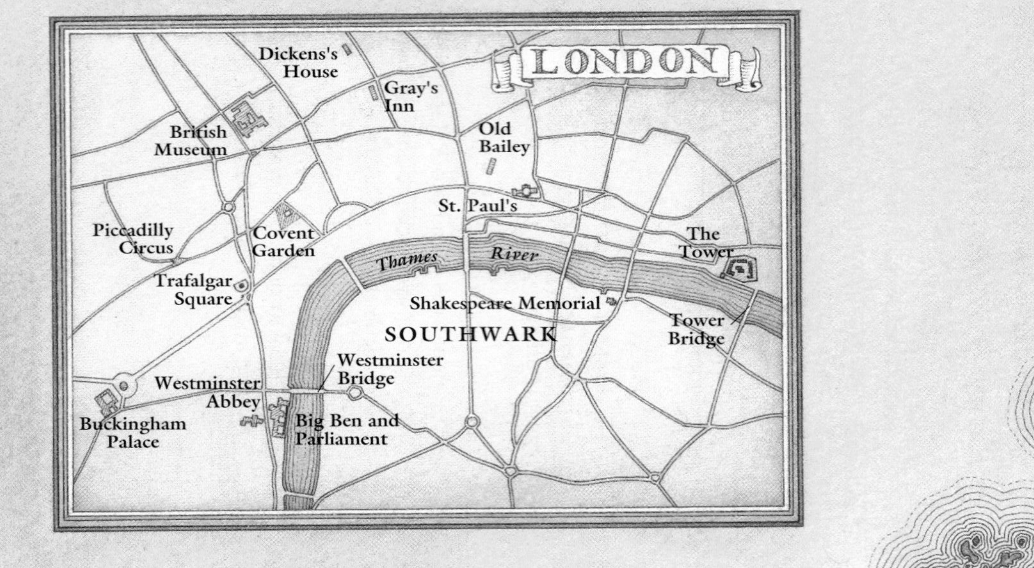

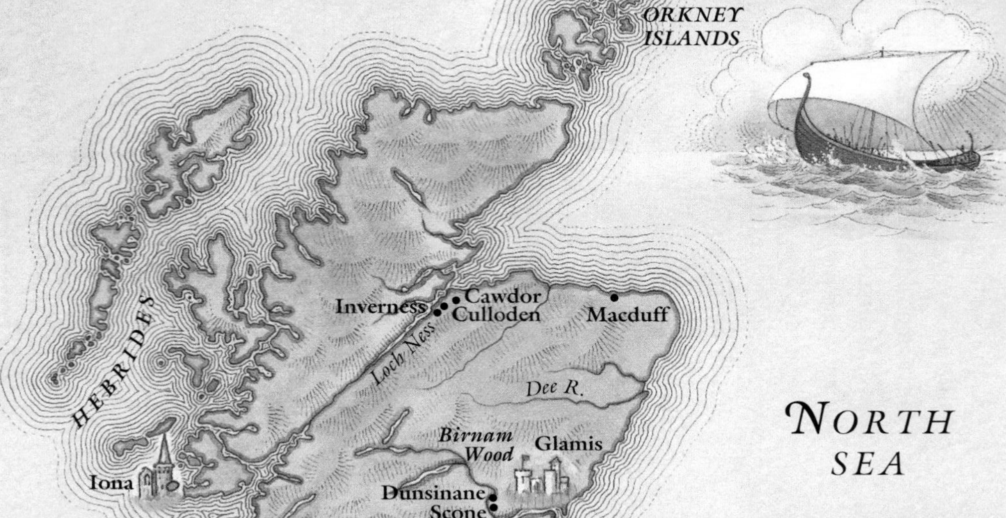

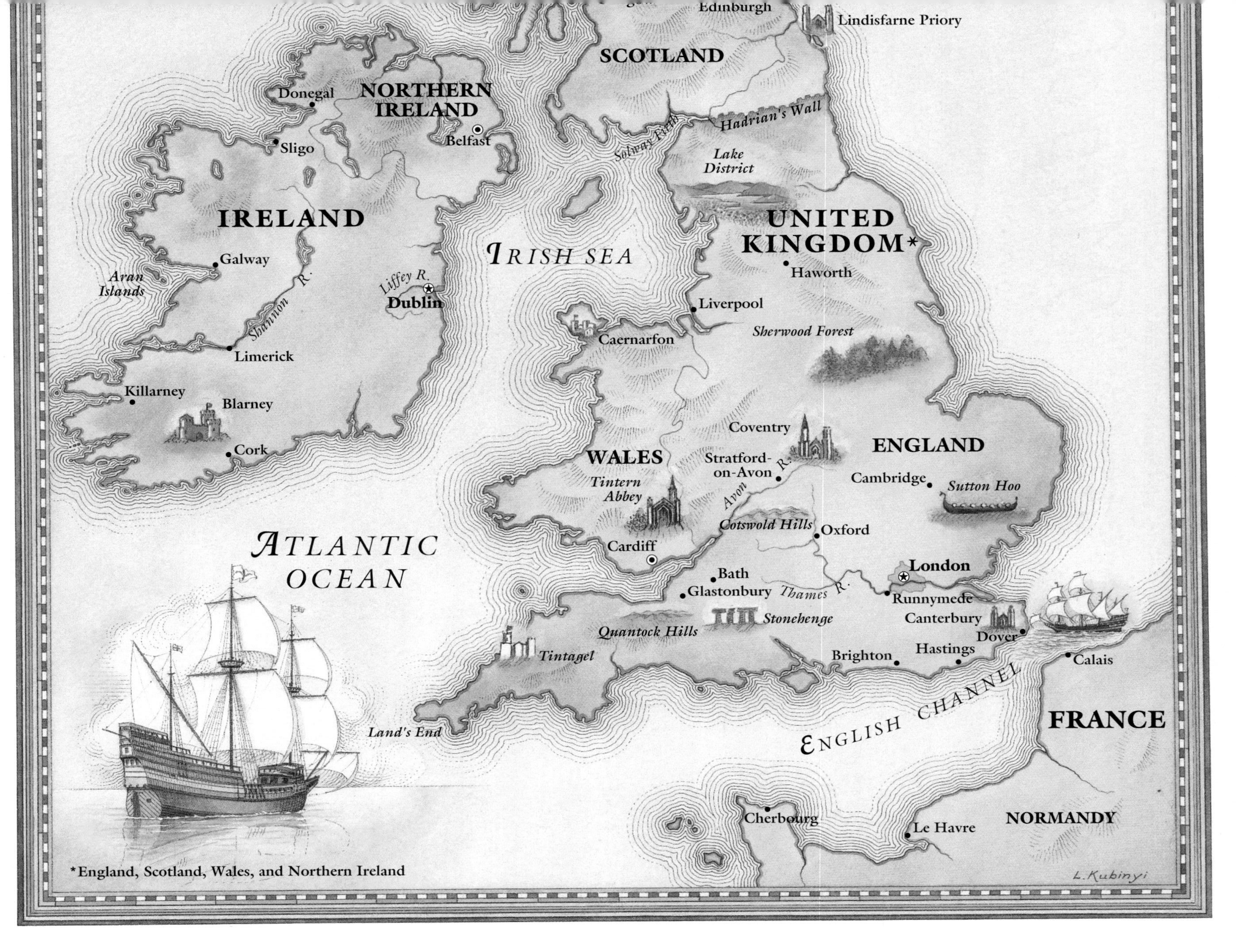
Edinburgh
Lindisfarne Priory
SCOTLAND
Donegal
NORTHERN IRELAND
Belfast
Sligo
Hadrian's Wall
Solway Firth
Lake District
IRELAND
UNITED KINGDOM*
Galway
Aran Islands
IRISH SEA
Haworth
Liffey R.
Dublin
Shannon R.
Liverpool
Limerick
Caernarfon
Sherwood Forest
Killarney
Blarney
Cork
Coventry
WALES
ENGLAND
Stratford-on-Avon
Avon R.
Tintern Abbey
Cambridge
Sutton Hoo
Cotswold Hills
Oxford
Cardiff
ATLANTIC OCEAN
London
Bath
Glastonbury
Thames R.
Runnymede
Stonehenge
Canterbury
Quantock Hills
Dover
Tintagel
Brighton
Hastings
Calais
Land's End
ENGLISH CHANNEL
FRANCE
Cherbourg
Le Havre
NORMANDY
*England, Scotland, Wales, and Northern Ireland
L. Kubinyi

Map of

NORTH AMERICA

Canada

United States

ATLANTIC OCEAN

CARIBBEAN SEA

St. Lucia

Trinidad and Tobago

PACIFIC OCEAN

SOUTH AMERICA

Chile

Argentina

the World
ARCTIC OCEAN
Russia
United Kingdom
Denmark
reland
Germany
EUROPE
Maginot Line
Ukraine
Russia
France
Croatia
Romania
Italy
MEDITERRANEAN SEA
Ancient Mesopotamia
Iraq
Iran
ASIA
China
Japan
Algeria
Egypt
Saudi Arabia
India
PACIFIC OCEAN
AFRICA
Nigeria
Liberia
Vietnam
ATLANTIC OCEAN
INDIAN OCEAN
Zimbabwe
South Africa
AUSTRALIA
New Zealand
L. Kubinyi

Invasion of Danes under Hinguar (Ingvar) and Hubba (detail). Page from *Life, Passion, and Miracles of St. Edmund* (c. 1130).